W9-BNU-761

WITHDRAWN

TRUE OR FALSE?

This person just shot a gun.

TRUE!

← microscopic residue

You can't see it, but every gun leaves its mark on the shooter. When a gun is fired, several chemicals from the explosion end up on the shooter's hand.

The gunshot residue, as it is called, doesn't stick to skin for long. If investigators have a suspected shooter, they have to act fast. They lift particles from the suspect's hand with sticky tape. They send that tape to the lab. There, it's tested for certain chemicals. If the test is positive, the police may have their shooter.

That's not all the clues guns leave behind. Experts can solve crimes with only a bullet as evidence.

Book design Red Herring Design/NYC

Library of Congress Cataloging-in-Publication Data
Joyce, Jaime, 1971–
Bullet proof! : the evidence that guns leave behind / by Jaime Joyce.
p. cm. — (24/7 : science behind the scenes)
Includes bibliographical references and index.
ISBN-13: 978-0-531-11820-7 (lib. bdg.)   978-0-531-15455-7 (pbk.)
ISBN-10: 0-531-11820-7 (lib. bdg.)   0-531-15455-6 (pbk.)
1. Forensic ballistics—Juvenile literature. 2. Forensic ballistics—United States— Case studies—
Juvenile literature. 3. Firearms—Identification—Case studies—Juvenile literature.
4. Bullets—Identification—Case studies—Juvenile literature. I. Title. II. Series.
HV8077.J69 2006
363.25'62—dc22   2006005718

FRANKLIN WATTS and associated logos are trademarks and/or registered
trademarks of Scholastic Library Publishing. SCHOLASTIC and associated logos
are trademarks and/or registered trademarks of Scholastic Inc.
1 2 3 4 5 6 7 8 9 10 R 16 15 14 13 12 11 10 09 08 07

BULLET PROOF!

The Evidence That Guns Leave Behind

Jaime Joyce

WARNING: All of the cases in this book are true. Many of the people profiled inside did not live to tell their own stories.

Franklin Watts®
A Division of Scholastic Inc.
New York • Toronto • London • Auckland • Sydney
Mexico City • New Delhi • Hong Kong
Danbury, Connecticut

CONTENTS

TRUE-LIFE CASE FILES!

These cases are 100% real. Find out how forensic firearms examiners solved these mysteries.

Gangsters are killed in this Chicago warehouse in 1929.

15 Case #1:
St. Valentine's Day Massacre

A gangland killing rocks the city of Chicago. Is it possible that the killers are police officers?

27 Case #2:
Caught in the Line of Fire

Can a few old cartridge cases help solve a ten-year-old murder case?

Police gather at the crime scene after a shooting.

35 Case #3:
Fired Up in Fairbanks

Someone is taking target practice—at cars and a government office. Can a firearms expert find the shooter?

Shots are fired at a government office in Fairbanks, AK.

5

FORENSIC DOWNLOAD

Shoot! Here's even more amazing stuff about forensic firearms examination.

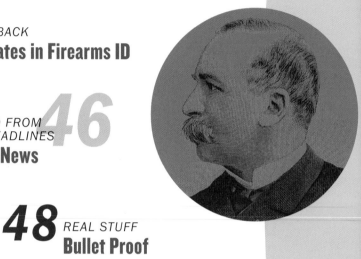
YELLOW PAGES

FORENSIC 411

Detectives arrive at a crime scene. There's a bullet stuck in the floor— but no gun in sight. Can a single bullet lead them to a criminal? That's a question for a forensic firearms expert.

Want to know what secrets a bullet holds? Don't shoot past these pages.

IN THIS SECTION:

- ▶ how forensic FIREARMS EXAMINERS really talk;
- ▶ how a GUN actually works;
- ▶ whom the firearms experts work with when they're ON THE JOB.

Ready, Aim, Talk!

Forensic firearms examiners have their own way of talking. Find out what their vocabulary means.

"I need someone from the forensic firearms identification team. Can we get anyone down here?"

forensic firearms identification
(fuh-REN-zik FYRE-armz eye-DEN-tih-fuh-KAY-shun)
the science of matching bullets and casings with the gun that fired them

"Wow, is that a bullet stuck in the wall?"

bullet
(BULL-it) a small missile, usually made of lead, that is fired from a gun

cartridge cases
(KAR-trij KAYSS-ez) metal cases that hold gunpowder and bullets inside a gun

"Put on some gloves, and see if you can find any cartridge cases on the floor."

8

"No, don't touch it! That bullet is evidence."

evidence
(EHV-uh-denss)
information used to prove innocence or guilt in a court of law

"Let's gather everything up and get it back to the **ballistics** lab. We'll see if we can get a **firearms** match there."

ballistics
(buh-LISS-tiks) the science and study of firearms and ammunition

firearms
(FYRE-armz) weapons that shoot bullets

Say What?

Here's some other lingo a forensic firearms examiner might use on the job.

hit
(hit) a match
*"The database gave us a **hit** on that gun you brought in. It was used in a robbery last year!"*

perp
(purp) a person who has committed a crime.
It's short for *perpetrator*.
*"It always feels good to send a **perp** to jail."*

bag
(bag) to take as evidence
*"**Bag** that casing. It might help us find the perp."*

Here's a view down the barrel of a gun. See the spiral pattern cut into it? That's called rifling. The indented parts of the pattern are called the grooves. The higher parts, between the grooves, are called the lands.

This rifling makes the bullets spin. They also help with firearms ID.

lands

The rifling in a barrel carves land and groove impressions into a bullet. Each type of gun leaves a different pattern.

Look at a bullet under a microscope, and you'll see tiny lines inside the lands and grooves. These lines are called striations. Suppose you have two guns that are exactly the same type. The lands and grooves from those guns will look the same. But every gun produces a different pattern of striations. That's how firearms experts match bullets with guns.

striations

firing pin imprint

grooves

Lasting Impressions

When a gun is fired, it leaves its mark on the bullet and the cartridge case. Those marks are the gun's fingerprints.

How does a gun leave a fingerprint? Here's how it works. A gun fires bullets. Each bullet sits inside a metal cartridge case. The cartridge case also holds gunpowder.

When a shooter pulls the trigger, the gun's **firing pin** hits the **primer**. The primer is the part of the cartridge that lights the gunpowder.

The gunpowder explodes. It pushes the bullet out of the cartridge case. The cartridge case is **ejected** from the gun. The bullet speeds through the barrel of the gun.

Inside the barrel is a series of **spiral** grooves called rifling. Rifling puts a spin on the bullet. The spin helps the bullet fly straight.

The rifling also carves marks into the bullet. Every gun is rifled in a slightly different way. That allows firearms examiners to trace a bullet to the kind of gun that fired it.

That's not all. Firearms experts also examine bullets under a microscope to look for striations. Those are tiny lines in the lands and grooves. They can help experts match a bullet to the exact gun from which it was shot.

Cartridge cases tell a story, just like bullets do. When a firing pin strikes the primer, it leaves a mark. Each type of gun leaves a different mark.

11

The Forensic Team

Forensic firearms examiners work as part of a team to help solve crimes.

POLICE OFFICERS
They are often the ones to find, collect, and transport the evidence. They sometimes take photos and give the forensic firearms examiners the crime scene data.

MEDICAL EXAMINERS
They're medical doctors who investigate suspicious deaths. They try to find out when and how someone died.

DETECTIVES
They direct the criminal investigation. They collect information about the crime, interview witnesses, identify suspects—and arrest them if there's enough evidence!

EVIDENCE TECHNICIANS
They label, store, and keep records of evidence. If bullets or casings are found at a crime scene, technicians make sure they are safely stored.

FORENSIC FIREARMS EXAMINERS
They are experts in the study of guns, bullets, and casings. They try to match bullets with the weapons that fired them.

ATTORNEYS
They are lawyers who argue criminal cases in court. District attorneys work for the state. They prosecute suspects. Defense lawyers defend suspects.

TRUE-LIFE CASE FILES!

24 hours a day, 7 days a week, 365 days a year, forensic firearms examiners are solving mysteries.

IN THIS SECTION:

▶ the mob almost frames Chicago POLICE for a crime;

▶ a gun helps to solve a ten-year-old MURDER CASE;

▶ a man ARRESTED for shooting at cars is linked to an attack on a government office.

Here's how forensic firearms examiners get the job done.

What does it take to solve a crime? Firearms experts don't just make guesses. They're like scientists. They follow a step-by-step process.

As you read the case studies, you can follow along with them. Keep an eye out for the icons below. They'll clue you in to each step along the way.

THE QUESTION At the beginning of a case, firearms examiners identify **one or two main questions** they have to answer.

THE EVIDENCE The next step is to **gather and analyze evidence**. Firearms examiners collect as much information as they can. Then they study it to figure out what it means.

THE CONCLUSION When they've studied all the data, firearms examiners **come to a conclusion**. What gun did a bullet or casing come from? If they can answer that question, they may have cracked the case.

St. Valentine's Day Massacre

A gangland killing rocks the city of Chicago. Is it possible that the killers are police officers?

Chicago, Illinois
February 14, 1929

A Bloody Valentine

Seven men are gunned down in cold blood. Were the killers really policemen?

February 14 is normally a day to celebrate love. On Valentine's Day 1929, the city of Chicago got murder instead.

At 10:30 A.M. a cold wind filled the air with snow. Seven men gathered in a red brick warehouse at 2122 North Clark Street. It was the Prohibition Era. No one had sold liquor legally in nine years. But some people made a fortune selling it illegally. And that's exactly what these men had in mind. They had been offered a shipment of illegal whiskey. The warehouse was their meeting place.

Outside in the snow, a police car pulled up. Four men got out and entered the warehouse. The sound of machine-gun fire rang out. A few minutes passed. The men reappeared. Two of them wore police uniforms and carried guns. The other two walked in front with their hands in the air. A woman who lived across the street had heard the gunfire. She looked out and **assumed** the police had caught some criminals.

Seven gangsters were shot in a warehouse in Chicago in 1929. At first, it seemed as though the Chicago police had committed the killings.

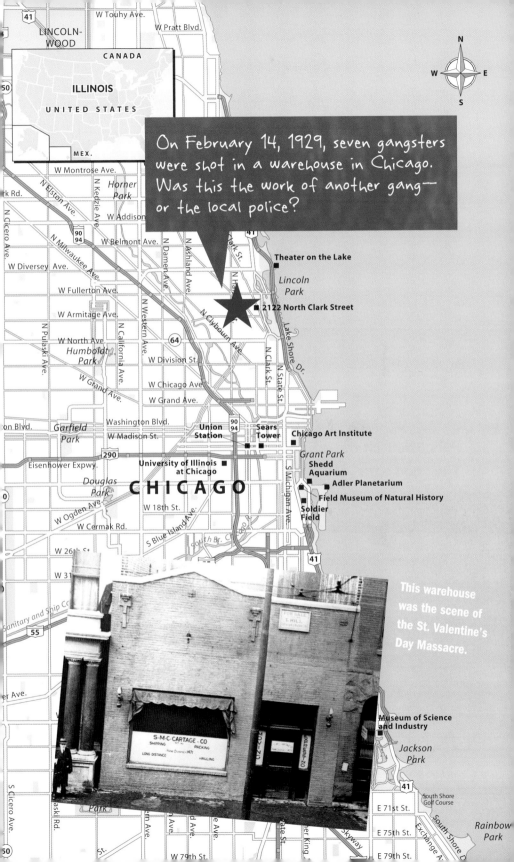

On February 14, 1929, seven gangsters were shot in a warehouse in Chicago. Was this the work of another gang—or the local police?

This warehouse was the scene of the St. Valentine's Day Massacre.

Theater on the Lake

2122 North Clark Street

Lincoln Park

Union Station

Sears Tower

Chicago Art Institute

University of Illinois at Chicago

Grant Park

Shedd Aquarium

Adler Planetarium

Field Museum of Natural History

Soldier Field

CHICAGO

Museum of Science and Industry

Jackson Park

South Shore Golf Course

Rainbow Park

CANADA

ILLINOIS

UNITED STATES

MEX.

LINCOLN-WOOD

However, if this was a police bust, it had gotten out of control. Neighbors heard a dog howling inside the warehouse. When they checked on the dog, they found a bloody mess. Seven men had been shot. All but one was dead—and he was failing fast.

In a day, the "St. Valentine's Day Massacre" would be all over the newspapers. The city of Chicago would be stunned. It's true that the victims were criminals. But did the police really shoot seven men and leave them to die?

Bagging the Bullets

Police search the crime scene for clues.
They come up with a theory and a lot of cartridge cases.

George "Bugs" Moran was the leader of the gang members who were killed in the massacre.

At the crime scene, police searched through the mess. It didn't take them long to identify the victims. The dead men were members of an organized crime gang led by George "Bugs" Moran.

Moran's gang controlled half the liquor trade in Chicago. Another gang, led by Al Capone, controlled the other half. Capone and Moran were rivals. Their gangs competed for business. Often the competition turned violent.

Were these gang murders? If so, why was there no evidence of a struggle? Police studied where the bodies had fallen. Moran's men had lined up willingly against the wall. Each one had been shot in the back.

Police quickly developed a theory. Capone became the main suspect. He was in Florida at the time. But police thought he had sent hired killers dressed as cops. The killers burst into the warehouse. Moran's men assumed it was a routine bust. They lined up against the wall. Then Capone's men opened fire.

Al Capone was the leader of a rival gang in Chicago. His nickname was "Scarface" because of the scar on his left cheek.

Here is the headline from the *New York Times* just after the Chicago murders. In the photo to the right, a crowd gathers as the police remove the bodies from the warehouse and place them in a wagon.

Still, police had to find the killers. And they had to make sure that there were no police officers involved.

The police focused on the physical evidence. The killers left no fingerprints behind. But they did leave a lot of evidence. There were 70 cartridge cases on the floor of the warehouse. Cartridge cases hold bullets and gunpowder. When a bullet is fired, the gun ejects the cartridge case.

Did the cases match guns used by the Chicago police? If not, what kind of gun did they come from? If the murder weapon turned up, could it be matched with the cases?

In 1929, there was one man who could answer all of these questions. Chicago police put in a call to Calvin Goddard.

THE GUN LAB

Calvin Goddard turns firearms identification into a science.

Police had 70 cartridge cases to work with in the St. Valentine's Day murders. A decade earlier, that wouldn't have meant much. Firearms examiners sometimes helped out in murder cases. But their work was not scientific. They didn't have a good way to compare bullets.

In 1923, a group of men decided to get scientific about firearms ID. A New York doctor named Calvin Goddard teamed with three others. Together they started the Bureau of Forensic Ballistics. At the bureau's lab they studied bullets.

Ballistics at Work

Goddard examines the casings.
Can he rule out the police as suspects?

Calvin Goddard arrived in Chicago. He was eager to help. The St. Valentine's Day Massacre was big news. All across the country, people were following the investigation in the papers. If Goddard helped solve the case, his work would be front-page news.

Goddard had two questions to answer. Were the bullets fired by police guns? If not, could they be matched with other weapons?

Calvin Goddard was one of the founders of the Bureau of Forensic Ballistics. Here, he is inspecting the rifling on the inside of the barrel of a gun.

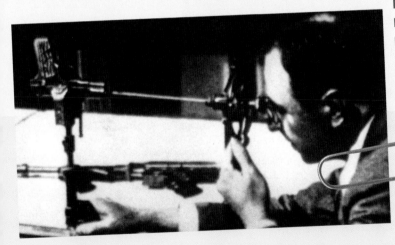

They **test-fired** every type of gun made. They recorded the markings on the bullets.

The lab also developed new tools. Goddard's partner, Philip Gravelle, invented the **comparison microscope**. Now, examiners could place images of two bullets side by side. That allowed them to see if the fine lines and markings matched.

By 1929, Goddard was the leading firearms expert in the U.S. Could he help crack Chicago's most famous murder case yet?

Goddard studied the cartridge cases from the warehouse. They came from .45-**caliber** Thompson **submachine guns**. Chicago police used these "Tommy guns." Then again, so did many of the gangsters in Chicago.

Goddard took a closer look at the cases. First, he took the eight machine guns owned by the Chicago police. He test-fired each one. He collected the cases. Then, he used a comparison microscope. He studied test-fired cases alongside the cases from the warehouse. None of the cases matched.

These two criminal investigators from 1945 are working with comparison microscopes. These microscopes allow investigators to compare bullets side by side. And they enlarge bullets 10–40 times their actual size.

Goddard announced his findings. The Chicago police were innocent.

That left one suspect: Al Capone. The people of Chicago wanted the truth. But they would have to wait. For now, police didn't have a clue.

A badge from 1931.

A ballistics expert fires a gun into a tub of water. He'll then analyze the markings that the gun leaves on bullets.

TESTING, 1-2-3

Here's how examiners catch a test-fired bullet—softly.

Firearms examiners often start with a bullet as evidence. Their job is to match the bullet with a gun. But they can't compare the two directly. They need a new bullet from the gun to match with the evidence on hand.

To get the bullet, examiners test-fire the gun. They don't want to damage the bullet. So they shoot into soft material. The first ballistics experts test-fired into thick wads of cotton. Today, examiners use tanks of water. Water doesn't mark up bullets. It also slows them down. That makes it easier to collect the fired bullets. A net on the outside of the tank (not shown) catches the cartridge cases.

Bulls-Eye!

The police find guns belonging to Capone's mob. Will the bullets match those guns?

For nearly a year, the investigation went nowhere. Capone had an **alibi** for Valentine's Day. So did Capone's main "hit man," Jack McGurn. McGurn was with his girlfriend at

THE CONCLUSION

Jack McGurn was Al Capone's main "hit" man. He was called Jack "Machine Gun" McGurn. The police suspected that he was involved in the massacre.

the time of the murders. Everyone in Chicago was convinced that Capone had ordered the hit. But no one could prove it.

In December, police got a break. Chicago police searched the home of a Capone hit man. They found two Thompson submachine guns. The guns were sent to Goddard's lab in New York. They were test-fired. Goddard then compared the cartridge cases to the ones found at the warehouse. He found one that matched perfectly.

Police pieced together the details of the story. Their theory had been right all along. Moran's men were lured to the warehouse by a call from Detroit. The caller promised a truck full of cheap whiskey. The killers did in fact dress as police officers.

Moran was the real target of the hit. Lucky for him, he arrived late. The killers were already there. Moran saw their car and left the scene.

In the end, police weren't able to **convict** the hit men or Al Capone. But the police finally caught up with Al Capone in 1931. They arrested him for cheating on his taxes.

It doesn't look high-tech, but it was in its day. This is Calvin Goddard's Scientific Crime Detection Laboratory. There, investigators used scientific methods to solve crimes. The lab was the first of its kind in the U.S.

Crime Lab

After working on the St. Valentine's Day case, Goddard opens an important new crime lab.

The real criminals behind the St. Valentine's Day Massacre went free. But Goddard's work on the case paid off. It proved to many people that crimes could be solved through science. Two people in particular noticed Goddard's work. They were businessmen in Chicago.

These men gave Goddard money to set up a

crime lab near Chicago. Goddard called it the Scientific Crime Detection Laboratory (SCDL). It was the first of its kind in the country. The SCDL didn't just deal with firearms ID. SCDL researchers studied fingerprints, handwriting, and blood. They analyzed evidence for police and spoke at trials.

SCDL also offered one of the first forensic training programs in the United States. An **FBI** agent named Charles Appel took classes there. In 1932, he went back to Washington and started the FBI's own crime lab.

Science was finding a permanent place in police work. For that we can thank one of the most famous criminals of all time: Al Capone. 24/7

Al Capone was finally arrested in 1931— not for murder, but for cheating on his taxes.

In the first case, forensic firearms ID was a new science. Today, computers make the process quicker and easier. Find out how in the next case.

Caught in the Line of Fire

Can a few old cartridge cases help solve a ten-year-old murder case?

Chicago, Illinois
September 30, 1995

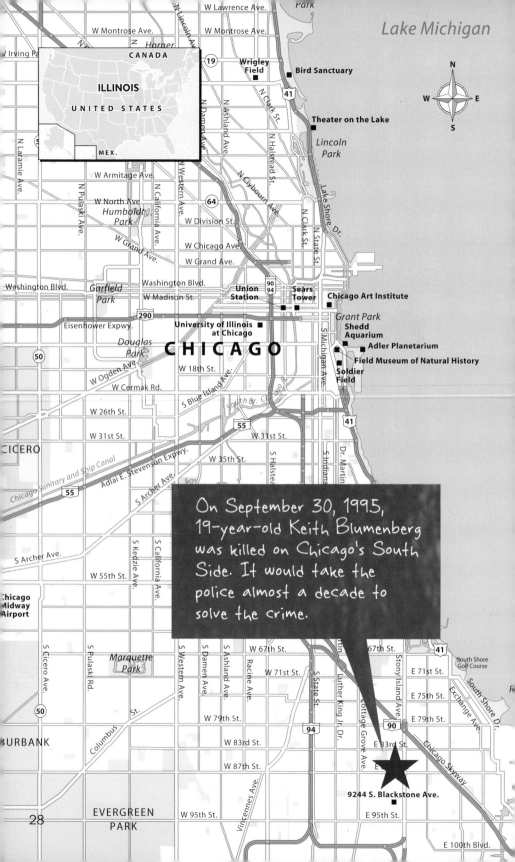

Lake Michigan

CANADA

ILLINOIS

UNITED STATES

MEX.

W Lawrence Ave.

W Montrose Ave.   W Montrose Ave.

Horner
Park

Wrigley
Field   Bird Sanctuary

Theater on the Lake

Lincoln
Park

W Armitage Ave.

W North Ave.   Humboldt
Park

W Division St.

W Chicago Ave.

W Grand Ave.   W Grand Ave.

Washington Blvd.   Garfield
Park

W Madison St.   Union
Station   Sears
Tower   Chicago Art Institute

Eisenhower Expwy.   University of Illinois
at Chicago   Grant Park   Shedd
Aquarium

Douglas
Park   CHICAGO   Adler Planetarium

W 18th St.   Field Museum of Natural History

W Cermak Rd.   Soldier
Field

W 26th St.

W 31st St.   W 31st St.

CICERO   W 35th St.

Adlai E. Stevenson Expwy.   S Archer Ave.

S Archer Ave.   W 55th St.

Chicago
Midway
Airport

Marquette
Park   W 67th St.   W 67th St.   South Shore
Golf Course

E 71st St.

W 71st St.   E 75th St.   South Shore Dr.

W 79th St.   E 79th St.

BURBANK   W 83rd St.   E 83rd St.

EVERGREEN
PARK   W 87th St.   Chicago Skyway

28   W 95th St.   E 95th St.

9244 S. Blackstone Ave.

E 100th Blvd.

On September 30, 1995,
19-year-old Keith Blumenberg
was killed on Chicago's South
Side. It would take the
police almost a decade to
solve the crime.

A Violent End

Keith Blumenberg was only 19 years old when he was shot and killed.

Keith Blumenberg loved music. His parents thought he was headed for a job as a disc jockey. At 19, he wasn't ready for that yet. He worked at a Solo Cup factory in Chicago. In his free time, he hung out with friends.

On September 30, 1995, Blumenberg got caught in the wrong place at the wrong time. That night he stood with five friends outside 9244 S. Blackstone Avenue. The neighborhood was a tough one on Chicago's South Side. Two rival gangs ruled the area.

As Blumenberg stood on the sidewalk, a black Nissan Pulsar pulled up. There were two men inside. One of them started shooting. A young man named Dameon Johnson took a bullet to the back. Another bullet hit Keith Blumenberg in the head. Police cars and ambulances rushed to the scene. Johnson survived the attack. Blumenberg did not.

The Nissan, meanwhile, disappeared into the night. Somehow, police had to find its trail.

Who killed Keith Blumenberg? There weren't many clues. But witnesses said the killer was driving a black Nissan.

On the Scene

The shooter left only bullets behind. Would they help police solve the case?

Police investigate a shooting. At the Chicago crime scene, the only physical evidence the police found were cartridge cases and some bullets. Would that be enough to find the killer?

Investigators roped off the crime scene. A crowd of people gathered outside the yellow tape.

The shooter hadn't left much evidence behind. He'd stayed in the car the entire time. That meant there were no footprints, no fingerprints, and no murder weapon.

The gun, however, had left some evidence. Police found six cartridge cases in the road. Police also found several bullets. The killer had shot into parked cars. Investigators dug the bullets out. Later, a medical examiner pulled a bullet from Blumenberg's skull. That was evidence, too.

Still, the investigation went nowhere. Several people had seen the shooting. But they were afraid of the gang members. No one would identify the killer. The evidence led to a dead end, too. Investigators searched but could not find the murder weapon. The case was unsolved.

[Forensic Fact]
In the U.S., murder is the #2 cause of death among people ages 15-24. More than 82% of these deaths are caused by guns.

WHAT'S AN IBIS?

Computer technology helps police track down suspects.

I BIS is a computer **database** that was developed in Canada. Its job is to match bullets and cartridge cases with weapons. Police departments in the U.S. started using it in 1995.

Police enter two kinds of information into **IBIS**. They enter images of bullets and cartridge cases found at crime scenes. They also enter data from guns found during criminal investigations. When police find a weapon, they fire it into a tank of water. They recover the bullets and photograph them. The information all goes into IBIS.

IBIS compares every new image with all the other images in the system. It scans the grooves, lands, and striations. It tries to match bullets with weapons. If it finds possible matches, it tells the user.

As of 2005, nearly a million pieces of data had been entered into IBIS. The system had produced more than 12,000 hits. Many of those hits led police straight to a suspect.

An investigator searches IBIS.

Heating Up

Can IBIS bring a cold case to life?

Almost exactly eight years passed after Keith Blumenberg's murder. Investigators had almost given up solving the case. Then, on September 28, 2003, Chicago police spotted a black Lincoln Town Car. Its rear window had been smashed. The officers pulled the car over. In the backseat, they found a loaded gun. It was a Glock Model 19

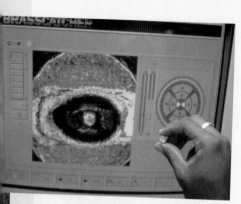

semiautomatic weapon. The officers seized the weapon.

Back at the station, the officers followed their normal routine. They handed the weapon over to the crime lab. The firearms examiners test-fired the gun. They collected the bullets and photographed them. They entered the evidence into IBIS.

IBIS found a match. The bullet that killed Keith Blumenberg had already been entered into IBIS. Marks on that bullet matched marks on the test-fired bullets from the Glock. It was June 2004 by then. A cold case was warming up.

There was just one problem. The people in the Lincoln Town Car had just bought the gun. They had nothing to do with the 1995 murder. Could police trace the gun to its owner eight years before?

IBIS includes software called "Brasscatcher." It helps law enforcement analyze cartridge cases. Here, a forensic expert compares markings on a cartridge case to an image from Brasscatcher.

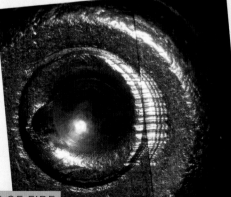

This cartridge case and firearm are a match. The marks made on the cartridge case (left) are the same as those on the firearm.

Tracking the Gun

IBIS gives investigators a lead. Will they be able to find the gun owner?

Three Chicago detectives teamed up with Jim Ferguson. He worked for the U.S. Bureau of Alcohol, Tobacco, Firearms and Explosives (ATF).

The four men began to trace the gun's history. The men in the Town Car had bought the gun from a drug user. He had stolen the gun from a family member. The family member got the gun from a gun trafficker. He got the gun in 1995, after Keith Blumenberg was killed.

Finally, police traced the weapon to a gun shop. A woman had bought the gun on September 29, 1995—the day before Blumenberg's murder. She bought the gun for a man named Samuel Coggs. The next day, Coggs borrowed the woman's car. At the time, she drove a black Nissan Pulsar.

THE EVIDENCE

An ATF agent at a crime scene.

A gun trafficker is someone who sells guns illegally.

DIGGING DEEP

Serial numbers on a gun can lead police to a killer.

One way to trace a gun's history is through its **serial number.** This number tells police who made the gun. That helps them track down the person who bought it.

Most criminals try to destroy the serial number. They file it down or punch holes over it so that it can't be seen. But the stamp goes much deeper than what can be seen on the surface. Firearms examiners use chemicals to "raise" the number. Examiners then take a picture of the serial number as evidence.

Case Closed

Investigators finally find the owner of the murder weapon.

At first, police didn't have enough evidence to arrest Coggs. Then, in November another witness came forward. She had seen the 1995 shooting. And she ID'd Samuel Coggs.

Six months later, investigators got another surprise. Coggs's passenger in the Nissan called the police. He said that Samuel Coggs was the shooter.

The next day, Coggs was arrested and charged with murder.

After the arrest, Detective Scott Rotkvich spoke to the *Chicago Sun Times*. "It was sweet to catch Coggs. He was still involved in illegal activities," he said. "Without that hit, this investigation would not have gone anywhere."

The arrest also helped Blumenberg's family. "I always thought they put it on the back burner," a relative told the *Chicago Sun Times*. "I never thought this would happen." 24/7

In this next case, no one was killed—fortunately. But a series of shootings left plenty of work for a forensic firearms expert.

Fired Up in Fairbanks

**Someone is taking target practice—
at cars and a government office.
Can a firearms expert find the shooter?**

Fairbanks, Alaska
November 24, 1995

Good Morning, Fairbanks

Someone fires shots at a government office.
Can science help catch the shooter?

It was a lazy Friday morning in Fairbanks, Alaska. Snow blanketed the ground. The sun was rising in the east.

Special Agent John Rayfield arrived for work just before 8:00 A.M. He opened the United States Fish and Wildlife Services (FWS) law enforcement office. He soon discovered that someone had fired two shots at the office. One went through a window,

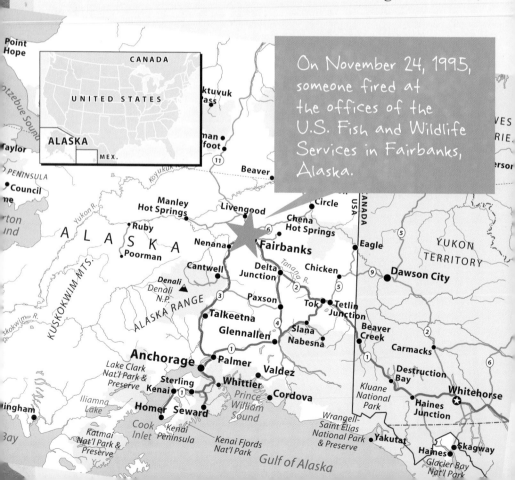

On November 24, 1995, someone fired at the offices of the U.S. Fish and Wildlife Services in Fairbanks, Alaska.

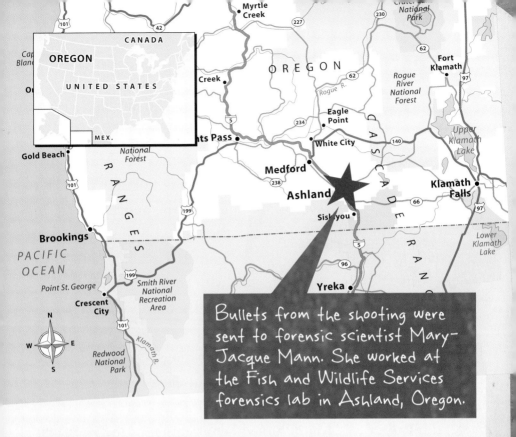

then through an inside wall. The other passed through the window seal. It landed on the floor of the office.

It didn't take long for Agent Rayfield to find the bullets. Rayfield packed them up. He sent them by mail to the FWS forensic lab in Ashland, Oregon. There, forensic scientist Mary-Jacque Mann would examine the evidence. Hopefully, she would be able to tell them what kind of weapon fired the shots.

One of the shots fired at the FWS office went through a window.

37

Searching for Clues

Mary-Jacque Mann takes note of all the details.

M.J. Mann at the U.S. Fish and Wildlife Service forensics laboratory in Ashland, Oregon. She was called in to help investigate the shootings in Fairbanks.

Mary-Jacque Mann had her hands full at FWS. Her lab was the only crime lab in the United States devoted to animals. Usually, Mann dealt with hunting and fishing crimes. She examined bullets and casings from illegal shootings. Grizzly bears and bald eagles were common victims of these crimes.

Mann turned her attention to the Fairbanks case. She had to find out what kind of gun fired the bullets.

The first step was to examine the bullets for **class characteristics**. Class characteristics are markings left on all bullets fired by a particular type of gun.

Mann looked at the number of lands and grooves. She used a tool called a **stage micrometer** to measure the distance between the lands and grooves. She entered this information into a database. The computer failed to pinpoint the exact type of gun. The bullets could have come from any one of 14 firearms.

Moving Targets

Police arrest a man for firing at cars.
Is he also the FWS shooter?

M.J. Mann sent her report to the Fairbanks police. For about a month, the investigation went nowhere. Then, on January 6, 1995, the Fairbanks police got a call. Someone was shooting at cars on the highway.

Police tracked down a man named Bradford A. Davis. He soon became a suspect in the FWS shooting. It was clear from his statements to police that Davis hated the government. The FWS is a government agency. Could his anger have led him to shoot at the office? Davis's gun, too, made him a possible suspect. It was a Colt M-1911 A1, one of the weapons listed in M.J. Mann's report.

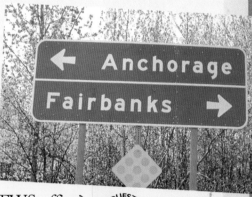

Was there a dangerous sniper on the loose in Fairbanks?

The pistol was the main piece of evidence in the case. Was this the gun used to shoot at the FWS office?

Police sent the Colt to a crime lab in Anchorage. Firearms examiners test-fired the weapon. They sent the test-fired bullets to Mann in Oregon.

Three days after Davis's arrest, an FWS trooper made another find. He used a metal detector outside the FWS office. There, under 20

BULLET IDENTIFICATION

Firearms examiners ask two kinds of questions: What type of gun did a bullet come from? And which gun was it fired from?

#1: CLASS CHARACTERISTICS

In many cases, bullets are recovered from a crime scene, but a weapon is not. When this happens, firearms examiners try to figure out what type of gun was used.

To do this, they look for class characteristics. Those are the markings that appear on all bullets fired by a particular type of gun. Examiners note the number of lands and grooves and the direction they twist. Examiners also measure the distance between the lands and grooves.

Then they enter the information into a computer database. The database tells them what type of gun makes those markings.

#2: INDIVIDUAL CHARACTERISTICS

Say the police get lucky. They find a weapon as well as bullets and cartridge cases. Then firearms examiners ask a different question. *Were these bullets and cartridge cases fired from this gun?*

To do this they test-fire the guns. Then they compare bullets. They look for striations on each bullet. These are the tiny lines inside the lands and grooves. Striations are like fingerprints. No two guns leave the same striations. If the individual characteristics match, examiners have their proof. The bullets were fired from the seized weapon.

[Forensic Fact]
Opened in 1988, the U.S. Fish and Wildlife Services Forensics Laboratory is still the only crime lab in the world working to solve crimes against animals.

inches (51 cm) of snow, he found two cartridge cases. He sent the cases to the Oregon lab.

M.J. Mann had everything she needed. First, she used a comparison microscope. She viewed the test-fired bullets next to the bullets found at the FWS office. She also compared the cartridge cases. Next, she examined the evidence using a powerful **scanning electron microscope**.

Mann reached a conclusion. The bullets found at the FWS office came from Bradford Davis's Colt pistol.

The Full Story

Who is Bradford Davis and what was his motive?

In February, John Rayfield and another agent met with Davis. The three men spoke at the prison in Fairbanks. Davis still hadn't confessed to the FWS shooting. And Rayfield wondered about his motive in shooting the cars. Davis hadn't hurt anyone. But he could have killed a driver. Was he a dangerous murderer at heart? Or just angry and disturbed?

During the meeting in the prison, the full story came out. Davis was originally from Pennsylvania. Life there got too busy for him. So he went on the road with his dog Busch.

BIG, BIGGER, BIGGEST
A high-tech tool zooms in on a bullet's tiniest markings.

The scanning electron microscope, or SEM, is a powerful tool. A standard microscope uses glass lenses to enlarge images. The SEM uses magnets and tiny particles called electrons.

The SEM produces extremely detailed images. A comparison microscope can enlarge a bullet to 10–40 times its actual size. The SEM can magnify tiny striations up to 10,000 times their actual size.

M.J. Mann says that's a big help when a case goes to trial. "Part of the examiner's job is to explain her work to the jury," she says. "The SEM produces vivid images that you can use in court to demonstrate the match."

Still, not many forensics labs are lucky enough to have SEMs. They're expensive and difficult to use. Most labs rely on a tool that hasn't changed much in 80 years—the comparison microscope.

Eventually, Davis and Busch settled in Alaska. They lived in a teepee near the Fairbanks FWS office. Then Busch was hit by a car and killed. Davis was heartbroken. He began to think that cars were evil. So he took out his anger by shooting at the highway. "I wanted to punish those cars," he said.

Davis eventually admitted that he shot at the FWS office. He explained that he hated the U.S. government. The FWS office was close to home. It made an easy target.

Police charged Davis with assault. In August 1997, he was convicted. But he never served his sentence. Before Davis went to jail, he was killed when his teepee caught fire. 24/7

Davis and his dog backpacked across the U.S. Then they settled in Alaska. They lived in a teepee like this one.

FORENSIC
DOWNLOAD

Firearms examination is all about the details. Check out even more details here.

IN THIS SECTION:

- ▶ TRACING forensic firearms identification into the past;
- ▶ why firearms ID is making HEADLINES;
- ▶ tools you can use to make BULLETS tell their story;
- ▶ whether FIREARMS EXAMINATION might be in your future!

Key Dates in

1835 The Butler Did It

Detective Henry Goddard investigates a burglary at a big house in England. The butler claims someone broke in and shot at him while he lay in bed. (A butler is a male servant.) Goddard pulls the bullet out of the headboard. He compares it to bullets from the butler's gun. They all show the same raised bump. The butler confesses. He robbed the house. Then he shot the gun to make it look like a break-in.

1889 Grooving

Forensic medicine professor Alexandre Lacassagne makes history. In Lyon, France, he matches the grooves on a bullet to the grooves in the barrel of a gun. Then he publishes his findings.

1926 Sacco and Vanzetti

Calvin Goddard uses a comparison microscope to examine evidence in a famous murder case. In 1920, two men robbed a shoe factory in Massachusetts. They killed two guards in the process. Two Italian immigrants, Nicola Sacco *(below left)* and Bartolomeo Vanzetti *(right)*, were convicted of the crime. Many Americans feel the two men are being treated unfairly. But Goddard links Sacco's gun to bullets from the crime scene. Sacco and Vanzetti are executed the following year.

Firearms ID

The science of firearms identification has been around since the 1800s. Take a look.

4

1929 No Love Lost

Killers dressed as police officers gun down seven men in Chicago. The killings become known as the St. Valentine's Day Massacre. Calvin Goddard uses firearms evidence to prove that Chicago police did not commit the murders.

See Case #1: St. Valentine's Day Massacre.

1930 Crime Lab

Calvin Goddard opens the Scientific Crime Detection Laboratory. It's located at Northwestern University in Evanston, Illinois. It is the first private lab of its kind in the U.S.

5

6

For more on IBIS, see page 31. see page 31.

1991 IBIS Is Born

A Canadian company begins work on the Integrated Ballistic Identification System (IBIS). This system uses computers to collect and compare images of bullets and casings.

1999 Wired!

The FBI and the U.S. Bureau of Alcohol, Tobacco, Firearms, and Explosives join forces. They create a nationwide program called **NIBIN**. The program provides police around the country with IBIS equipment. In six years, nearly a million pieces of information have been entered into the system. Police have made more than 12,000 hits.

7

In the News

Read all about it! Forensic firearms identification is in the news.

Above: The suspects were arrested at a highway rest stop. Here, forensic investigators get ready to search the suspects' van. *Left:* The FBI used metal detectors to search for firearms evidence after a sniper shooting near Washington, D.C.

Suspects' Rifle Linked to Sniper Attacks

ROCKVILLE, MARYLAND—October 25, 2002

For three weeks, sniper attacks terrorized the Washington, D.C., area. Ten people were killed and three wounded.

On October 24, two men were arrested for the killings. The suspects were John Allen Muhammad and Lee Boyd Malvo. A rifle was seized from the suspects' car.

Now, CNN.com reports that bullets used in 11 of the shootings were traced to the rifle. "We have the weapon," announced Montgomery County police chief Charles Moose. "It is off the streets."

Stamping Out Crime

BOSTON—July 27, 2006

In July 2006, Boston Mayor Thomas Menino presented the new plan to use microstamping to help identify guns.

According to CBS News, Boston police support a new way to identify guns. The process is called microstamping.

Microstamping uses lasers to etch information onto a gun's firing pin. The information would include the gun's make, model, and serial number. The firing pin then stamps the information onto a casing each time the gun is fired.

IBIS Leads to Murder Conviction

OXON HILL, MARYLAND—April 2, 2005

Evidence from a ballistics database helped convict a Maryland man of murder yesterday.

Last April, 22-year-old Kelvin Braxton was eating in a fast-food restaurant. Robert Garner, 20, walked in. Braxton refused to shake Garner's hand. The two argued. Garner later shot Braxton outside the restaurant.

Police found ten cartridge cases at the crime scene. They entered images of the cases into IBIS. The computer database matched the cases with a cartridge case already on file. This case was from a gun recently bought by Garner's girlfriend.

Garner will be sentenced in May of this year.

47

Bullet Proof

Have a look at the tools, equipment, forms, and other stuff used by a forensic firearms examiner.

Every ballistics report is different. But they all serve a similar purpose. They tell judges and juries about gun-related evidence found at a crime scene. If a gun was found, was it the gun used to commit a crime? If no gun was found, what kind of gun could have fired the bullets?

This is a real ballistics report used in a case.

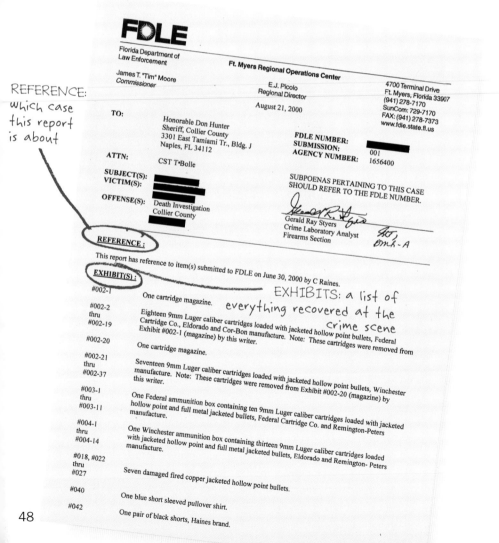

REFERENCE: which case this report is about

FDLE

Florida Department of Law Enforcement

James T. "Tim" Moore
Commissioner

Ft. Myers Regional Operations Center

E.J. Picolo
Regional Director

4700 Terminal Drive
Ft. Myers, Florida 33907
(941) 278-7170
SunCom: 729-7170
FAX: (941) 278-7373
www.fdle.state.fl.us

August 21, 2000

TO:
Honorable Don Hunter
Sheriff, Collier County
3301 East Tamiami Tr., Bldg. J
Naples, FL 34112

FDLE NUMBER:
SUBMISSION:
AGENCY NUMBER: 001
1656400

ATTN: CST T·Bolle

SUBJECT(S):
VICTIM(S):

SUBPOENAS PERTAINING TO THIS CASE
SHOULD REFER TO THE FDLE NUMBER.

OFFENSE(S): Death Investigation
Collier County

Gerald Ray Styers
Crime Laboratory Analyst
Firearms Section

REFERENCE :

This report has reference to item(s) submitted to FDLE on June 30, 2000 by C Raines.

EXHIBIT(S) :

EXHIBITS: a list of everything recovered at the crime scene

#002-1
One cartridge magazine.

#002-2
thru
#002-19
Eighteen 9mm Luger caliber cartridges loaded with jacketed hollow point bullets, Federal Cartridge Co., Eldorado and Cor-Bon manufacture. Note: These cartridges were removed from Exhibit #002-1 (magazine) by this writer.

#002-20
One cartridge magazine.

#002-21
thru
#002-37
Seventeen 9mm Luger caliber cartridges loaded with jacketed hollow point bullets, Winchester manufacture. Note: These cartridges were removed from Exhibit #002-20 (magazine) by this writer.

#003-1
thru
#003-11
One Federal ammunition box containing ten 9mm Luger caliber cartridges loaded with jacketed hollow point and full metal jacketed bullets, Federal Cartridge Co. and Remington-Peters manufacture.

#004-1
thru
#004-14
One Winchester ammunition box containing thirteen 9mm Luger caliber cartridges loaded with jacketed hollow point and full metal jacketed bullets, Eldorado and Remington- Peters manufacture.

#018, #022
thru
#027
Seven damaged fired copper jacketed hollow point bullets.

#040
One blue short sleeved pullover shirt.

#042
One pair of black shorts, Haines brand.

48

#044   One pair of pink night shorts.

#045   One pink nightshirt, Delicates brand.

#056   One fired 9mm Luger caliber cartridge case, Federal Cartridge Co. manufacture.

#069   One extremely damaged copper fragment.

#070   One extremely damaged lead fragment.

#071   One extremely damaged copper fragment.

#076   One damaged lead bullet core.

#077   One damaged fired copper bullet jacket.

#078   One damaged fired copper jacketed bullet.

#079 thru #089   Eleven fired 9mm Luger caliber cartridge cases, Eldorado and Federal Cartridge Co. manufacture.

#108   One damaged fired copper jacketed bullet.

RESULTS: what the evidence means or shows. Which bullets match which guns?

RESULT(S):

Exhibits #018, #022 through #027, #077, #078 and #108 are fired 9mm Luger caliber copper jacketed hollow point bullets and a copper bullet jacket. These exhibits display polygonal style rifling six in number, right twist. This style of rifling is consistent with firearms manufactured by Glock, Heckler & Koch, Kahr and others. Any suspect firearm should be submitted for comparison purposes.

Exhibits #022, #023, #027, #077, #078 and #108 were identified as having been fired from the same firearm.

Exhibits #018, #024 through #026 could neither be identified nor eliminated as having been fired from the same firearm, which fired Exhibits #022, #023, #027, #077, #078 and #108.

Exhibits #056 and #079 through #089 were identified as having been fired in the same firearm.

Exhibit #002-25 (cartridge) from cartridge magazine, Exhibit #002-20, revealed ramp feed marks on the body of the cartridge case near the mouth. These markings were identified to the same markings appearing on the body of Exhibits #056, #079, #080, #081 and #84 through #088. This conclusion shows that these Exhibits had been in contact with the same feed ramp and chambered into the same firearm.

Exhibits #082, #083 and #089 did not have any ramp feed marks present.

Exhibits #002-1 and #002-20 are designed to hold 9mm Luger caliber cartridges and fit into Glock manufactured pistols.

Exhibit #040 revealed three holes in the front central area and one hole in upper back central area. The area around holes in the front and back were examined microscopically and processed chemically for the presence of gunpowder and/or lead residues and some residues were noted on the front only. Due to the absence of a firearm for testing no meaningful muzzle-to-garment distance can be given.

Exhibit #042, #044 and #045 revealed no holes/defects.

Exhibit #076 is a lead bullet core of caliber 38 class that includes 9mm Luger caliber.

Exhibits #069, #070 and #071 are of no value for examination.

Exhibits #002-2 through #002-19, #002-21 through #002-37, #003-2 through #003-11 and #004-2 through #004-14 are suitable for use in a 9mm Luger caliber pistol.

A video image of Exhibit #087 has been entered into the Florida NIBIN/Drugfire Database as Case #21736. This image will be compared with those images of cartridge cases and firearms recovered in other incidents. Your agency will be notified of any future results.

REMARK(S):

The submitted exhibit (s) should be picked up at your earliest convenience. If this is not feasible, please contact the Evidence Section at (941) 278-7170, ext. 153 to make other arrangements.

REMARKS: any extra information about the case or evidence

comparison microscope

A firearms examiner's main tool. It has two sets of lenses to enlarge images. That allows firearms inspectors to compare two bullets at the same time.

lenses

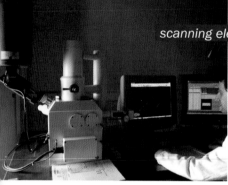

scanning electron microscope (SEM)

A microscope that produces extremely detailed images. A comparison microscope can enlarge a bullet to 10–40 times its actual size. The SEM can magnify tiny striations up to 10,000 times their actual size. The SEM uses magnets and tiny particles called electrons.

trigger-pull gauge

This device shows how much force it takes to pull a trigger. Police use it when a suspect says the "gun just went off." If the trigger is hard to pull, the suspect is probably lying.

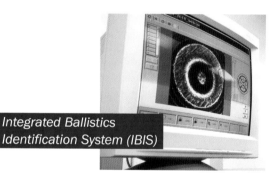

Integrated Ballistics Identification System (IBIS)

IBIS is a computer database that stores images of bullets and cartridge cases. When police find new evidence, they enter it into the database. IBIS tries to match it with evidence already in the system.

disposable rubber gloves
Firearms examiners use chemicals to restore serial numbers on guns. They wear rubber gloves to protect their hands.

water tank Firearms examiners test-fire guns into huge tanks of water. The water slows the bullets down—without leaving any marks. Most tanks have a net on the outside that catches the cartridge cases. Here, an examiner shows a bullet she pulled from a water tank. She'll analyze the markings the gun she tested made on this bullet.

scale Small scales are sometimes used to weigh bullets. A bullet's weight helps determine its caliber.

headphones Test-firing guns is like setting off firecrackers inches from your head. Firearms examiners wear headphones to protect their ears from the noise.

calipers This tiny tool measures the land and groove marks on a bullet. The results help determine a gun's caliber. They also suggest what type of gun the bullet came from.

boots and coveralls Sometimes, firearms examiners collect evidence at crime scenes. When they do, they often wear protective clothing. This is a covering for a shoe.

51

HELP WANTED:
Forensic Firearms Examiner

Would you like to take a shot at a career as a forensic firearms examiner? Here's more information about this field.

Q&A: MARY-JACQUE MANN

Mary-Jacque Mann is a forensic firearms examiner at the U.S. Fish and Wildlife Forensic Laboratory in Ashland, Oregon.

24/7: What's your favorite thing about being a forensic firearms examiner?

MANN: The search, getting something that was a complete unknown and discovering its secrets.

24/7: What advice would you give to young people interested in a career as a forensic firearms examiner?

MANN: Think about science, not Hollywood. It's really not a glamorous job. You need a good foundation in science and a scientific attitude. Steer away from the "CSI syndrome." Crime scenes are not like that.

24/7: What can young people do now to get involved in the field?

MANN: Invite a local crime lab to a Career Day. State and local crime labs will come out for free to talk with students about careers in forensic science.

24/7: Forensic firearms identification sounds really cool. What do you have to do to get a job?

MANN: Well, you'll have to graduate from high school first. And you'll need good grades to get into college!

Every state is different, but most police departments and crime labs want you to have a four-year college degree. You will need to earn a degree in criminal justice, industrial technology, physical science, or a related field. You will also have to complete training courses.

The New York City Police Department now requires forensic firearms examiners to have a master's degree. This means you will have to spend at least two more years in college.

Finally, for now, read everything you can about the profession.

24/7: How do you know if you'd be a good firearms examiner?

MANN: Good forensic firearms examiners pay attention to detail. And they must be comfortable handling firearms. They must also be able to speak and write well. Speaking as an expert witness in court and writing reports are part of the job.

Forensic firearms examiners must also examine evidence carefully. New technology has been developed that can help us with our work. But computers cannot do the work alone.

THE STATS

MONEY
▶ Salaries are different depending on where you live. The starting salary in Kentucky is $22,000. The starting salary in Fort Worth, Texas, is $42,598.

EDUCATION
Forensic firearms examiners must finish the following:
▶ 4 years of college OR
▶ 4 years of experience in a forensics lab
▶ 2 years of on-the-job training
▶ New York state requires 2 years of graduate school in forensic science

Take this totally unscientific quiz to find out if forensic firearms examination might be a good career for you.

1 **How do you feel about speaking in front of lots of people?**
a) You can't shut me up!
b) I can do it pretty well, but I'd rather not.
c) I'd rather dig ditches on the hottest summer day!

2 **Do you pay attention to details?**
a) Yes, I could find a needle in a haystack.
b) I'm pretty good, but I like for someone else to point stuff out, too.
c) Hello? Did you see me just walk into that street sign?

3 **Do you get grossed out?**
a) The grosser the better for me!
b) I don't mind the sight of blood—as long as it's not mine!
c) Don't even tell me what you have in mind!

4 **Are you interested in science?**
a) Yes, my science classes are my favorite.
b) It's pretty interesting.
c) I just can't seem to understand it.

5 **Do you like technology?**
a) It's really cool. I love learning the latest about computers.
b) It's OK. I can work with it when I need to.
c) How do you turn this computer on again?

YOUR SCORE

Give yourself 3 points for every "**a**" you chose. Give yourself 2 points for every "**b**" you chose. Give yourself 1 point for every "**c**" you chose.

If you got **13–15 points**, you'd probably be a good forensic firearms examiner. If you got **10–12 points**, you might be a good forensic firearms examiner. If you got **5–9 points**, you might want to look at another career!

HOW TO GET STARTED...NOW!

It's not too early to start working toward your goals.

GET AN EDUCATION

▶ Focus on your science classes, such as physics and chemistry.

▶ Start thinking about college. Look for ones with good physical, biological, or forensic science programs.

▶ Read the newspaper. Keep up with what's going on in your community.

▶ Read anything you can find about ballistics. See the books and Web sites in the Resources section on pages 56–58.

▶ Graduate from high school!

NETWORK!

▶ Find out about forensic groups in your area. See if you can find a local forensic firearms examiner who might be willing to give you advice.

GET AN INTERNSHIP

▶ Look for an internship with a firearms examiner.

▶ Look for an internship in a local forensics lab.

LEARN ABOUT OTHER JOBS IN THE FIELD

There are many jobs related to firearms examination, including:

▶ police officer
▶ forensic chemist
▶ crime scene analyst
▶ crime scene technician
▶ crime lab supervisor

A firearms expert holds an oversized model of a bullet.

Resources

Looking for more information about forensic firearms identification? Here are some resources you don't want to miss!

PROFESSIONAL ORGANIZATIONS

Bureau of Alcohol, Tobacco, Firearms and Explosives (ATF)
www.atf.treas.gov/explarson/itoolmark.htm
650 Massachusetts Avenue, NW
Washington, DC 20226
PHONE: 202-927-9380
This government agency is dedicated to preventing violent crime and protecting the U.S. On its Web site, click on "Other Programs," then "Training" to learn about firearms-related training sessions at the National Firearms Examiner Academy.

California Criminalistics Institute (CCI)
http://www.cci.ca.gov/
4949 Broadway, Room A104
Sacramento, CA 95820
FAX: 916-454-5433
The CCI provides forensic training to scientists already in the field. Visit this site to see a class schedule and read course descriptions.

Canadian Society of Forensic Science/La Société Canadienne des Sciences Judiciaires (CSFS)
www.csfs.ca
P.O. Box 37040
3332 McCarthy Road
Ottawa, Ontario
Canada K1V 0W0
PHONE: 613-738-0001
FAX: 613-738-1987
Visit the CSFS Web site, or write to their headquarters for information about forensic science training programs in Canada.

Federal Bureau of Investigation (FBI)
http://www.fbi.gov/hq/lab/org/ftu.htm
J. Edgar Hoover Building
935 Pennsylvania Avenue, NW
Washington, DC 20535-0001
PHONE: 202-324-3000
The FBI is a government agency that investigates major crimes. This page from its Web site focuses on the Firearms-Toolmark Unit of the FBI Laboratory.

**U.S. Fish and Wildlife Service
National Fish and Wildlife
Forensic Laboratory**
http://www.lab.fws.gov/
1490 E. Main Street
Ashland, OR 97520
PHONE: 541-482-4191
FAX: 541-482-4989
Want to learn more about what it's
like to work in a forensic crime lab
that's dedicated to solving crimes
against wildlife? Check out this site,
or contact the lab by mail or by phone.

WEB SITES

American Association of Crime Lab Directors (ASCLD)
www.ascld.org
On the ASCLD home page, click on "Visitors," then "Educational/ Academics" for answers to frequently asked questions about what it takes to become a forensic scientist. You can also click on "Forensic Links" for a comprehensive listing of forensic science Web sites.

Association of Firearm and Tool Mark Examiners (ATFE)
www.afte.org
Go to this site for forensic links and information about the annual AFTE conference.

Careers in Forensic Science
www.forensicdna.com/ careers/htm
This site gives an overview of requirements and options for careers in forensic science.

Court TV's Crime Library
www.crimelibrary.com
This site has lots of information about crime and forensic science.

Firearms ID
www.firearmsID.com
This site presents detailed information about forensic firearms identification.

BOOKS ABOUT FORENSIC SCIENCE

Camenson, Blythe. *Opportunities in Forensic Science Careers.* New York: McGraw-Hill, 2001.

Fisher, Barry A. J. *Techniques of Crime Scene Investigation,* 7th ed. Boca Raton, Fla.: CRC Press, 2003.

Genge, Ngaire, E. *The Forensic Casebook: The Science of Crime Scene Investigation.* New York: Ballantine, 2002.

Platt, Richard. *Ultimate Guide to Forensic Science.* New York: DK Publishing, 2003.

Ramsland, Katherine M. *The Forensic Science of CSI.* New York: Berkley Trade, 2001.

Rudin, Norah, and Keith Inman. *An Introduction to Forensic Analysis,* 2nd ed. Boca Raton, Fla.: CRC Press, 2001.

COLLEGES

Only a few schools offer a full-fledged undergraduate degree in forensic science. A greater number allow a minor or concentration in forensic science along with a degree in one of the physical sciences. Here is a selection of colleges to consider, and some of these offer master's degree programs as well:

Albany State University
www.asurams.edu
Forensic Science
Department of Criminal Justice
504 College Drive
Albany, GA 31705
PHONE: 229-430-4864

George Washington University
www.gwu.edu
Graduate Programs
Department of Forensic Sciences
2036 H Street
Samson Hall
Washington, DC 20052
PHONE: 202-994-7319

John Jay College of Criminal Justice
www.jjay.cuny.edu
Forensic Science
889 Tenth Avenue
New York, NY 10019
PHONE: 212-237-8000

Virginia Commonwealth University
www.vcu.edu
Forensic Science
College of Humanities and Sciences
P.O. Box 843079
Richmond, VA 23284
PHONE: 804-828-8420

A

alibi (AL-uh-bye) *noun* proof that an accused person was somewhere else when a crime occurred

assume (uh-SOOM) *verb* to suppose that something is true, without checking it

B

bag (bag) *verb* to take as evidence

ballistics (buh-LISS-tiks) *noun* the science and study of firearms and ammunition

barrel (BAH-ruhl) *noun* the long part of a gun that looks like a tube

bullet (BULL-it) *noun* a small missile, usually made of lead, that is fired from a gun

C

caliber (KAL-uh-bur) *noun* the inner width of a gun barrel. It is the distance between the opposite lands, which are the raised parts of the spiral inside the barrel of a gun.

cartridge (KAR-trij) *noun* a unit of ammunition. It includes the case, primer, gunpowder, and bullet.

cartridge case (KAR-trij kayss) *noun* the outside of a cartridge. Sometimes called shell or shell casing.

casing (KAYSS-ing) *noun* the outside of a cartridge. A shortened version of *cartridge case.*

class characteristics (klas ka-rik-tuh-RISS-tiks) *noun* markings left on all bullets fired by a particular type of gun

comparison microscope (kuhm-PAIR-uh-sun MYE-kruh-skope) *noun* a microscope with two lenses, which allow firearms examiners to compare two bullets side by side

convict (kun-VIKT) *verb* to prove that someone is guilty of a crime

D

database (DA-tuh-bayss) *noun* a large collection of information that is organized and stored on a computer

E

eject (ih-JEKT) *verb* to push something out, sometimes by force

Dictionary

electron (ih-LEK-tron) *noun* a tiny particle in an atom. Electrons have a negative electrical charge.

evidence (EHV-uh-denss) *noun* materials, facts and details collected from a crime scene that may help solve a crime

expert (EX-purt) *noun* a person who knows a lot about a certain field. See page 12 for a list of forensic experts.

F

FBI (EF-bee-eye) *noun* a U.S. government agency that investigates major crimes. It stands for *Federal Bureau of Investigation*.

firearm (FYRE-arm) *noun* a weapon that shoots bullets

firing pin (FYRE-ing pin) *noun* a pin inside a firearm that strikes the cartridge primer

forensic (fuh-REN-zik) *adjective* relating to scientific evidence used in legal cases

forensic firearms identification (fuh-REN-zik FYRE-armz eye-DEN-tih-fuh-KAY-shun) *noun* the science of matching bullets and cartridge casings with the gun that fired them

G

groove (groov) *noun* a cut in the surface of a bullet

H

hit (hit) *noun* a match. Also gangster slang for a planned murder.

I

IBIS (EYE-bis) *noun* a computer database used to collect and compare firearm evidence. It stands for *Integrated Ballistics Identification System*.

ID (eye-DEE) *noun* the process of figuring out who or what something is. It is short for *identification*.

L

land (land) *noun* the raised area between grooves on a bullet

N

NIBIN (NIH-bin) *noun* a program that provides police around the country with IBIS equipment. It stands for *National Integrated Ballistics Identification Network*.

P

perp (purp) *noun* a person who has committed a crime. It is short for *perpetrator*.

primer (PRY-muhr) *noun* a cap in a bullet cartridge that contains gunpowder

R

rifling (RYE-fling) *noun* the series of land and groove marks inside the barrel of a gun

S

scanning electron microscope (SKAN-ing uh-LEK-tron MYE-kro-skope) *noun* a microscope that produces extremely detailed images

semiautomatic (se-MEE-awh-tuh-MA-tik) *adjective* describing a gun that can fire repeatedly

serial number (SEER-ee-yul NUHM-bur) *noun* like a license plate for cars, a serial number is etched onto a gun's surface. It is used to identify the gun's owner.

spiral (SPYE-ruhl) *adjective* a kind of pattern that winds around in circles like a spring

stage micrometer (stayj mye-KROM-muh-tur) *noun* a tool that measures the distance between a bullet's grooves and lands

striations (stry-AY-shuns) *noun* tiny lines found inside the lands and grooves on a bullet. They are created as the bullet passes through the barrel of a gun. They can only be seen with a microscope.

submachine gun (suhb-muh-SHEEN gun) *noun* an automatic gun fired from a person's hip or shoulder

T

test-fire (test-FYRE) *verb* to shoot a firearm in order to gain information about its bullets

Index

Sometimes, teachers tell you to "write about what you know." Me? I like to write about the things I *don't* know. By the time I'm finished, I've learned a lot about a fascinating subject.

That's what happened with this book. It required a lot of research. I started by reading as much as I could about forensic firearms identification. That way, when it came time to talk to forensic firearms examiners, I knew what kind of questions to ask. And I could understand their answers!

As part of my research, I also visited the Firearms Analysis Unit of the New York City Police Department. This was really helpful because I was able to see a real-life crime lab in action. I put on headphones as an examiner test-fired a gun into a steel tank full of 750 gallons of water. I looked through a comparison microscope. And I talked to an examiner in the lab about how he used the IBIS machine.

So, by the time I was done with all of my research, I guess I really was writing about what I know. It just took a while to get there.

ACKNOWLEDGMENTS

I would like to thank the following individuals for talking with me about their work in the field of forensic firearms identification. Without their help, this book would not be possible.

Sergeant Keith Bavolar, Firearms Analysis Unit, New York City Police Department, Queens, New York

Scott Doyle, Firearms and Toolmark Examiner, Kentucky State Police, Jefferson Regional Lab, Jefferson, Kentucky

Mary-Jacque Mann, Forensic Firearms Examiner, ISS Consulting

John Rayfield, U.S. Fish and Wildlife Service

Darrell Stein, Firearm Examiner, Houston Police Department, Houston, Texas

CONTENT ADVISER: H. W. "Rus" Ruslander, Forensic Supervisor, Palm Beach County (Florida) Medical Examiner's Office